SCHIRMER'S LIBRARY
OF MUSICAL CLASSICS

Vol. 1898

BENEDETTO MARCELLO

Six Sonatas
For Cello or Double Bass and Piano

Keyboard Realization and
Cello part edited by
ANALEE BACON

Double Bass part edited by
LUCAS DREW

ISBN 978-0-7935-5180-4

G. SCHIRMER, Inc.

DISTRIBUTED BY

HAL•LEONARD®
CORPORATION
7777 W. BLUEMOUND RD. P.O. BOX 13819 MILWAUKEE, WI 53213

Six Sonatas

for Violoncello (or Bass) and Piano

Solo Bass Part
edited by Lucas Drew

Benedetto Marcello
(1686 ~ 1739)
Keybord Realization
and Violoncello Part
edited by Analee Bacon

Sonata 1

Copyright © 1973 by G. Schirmer, Inc. (ASCAP) New York, NY
International Copyright Secured. All Rights Reserved.

47217 cx

Sonata 2

Adagio

Allegro

Allegro moderato

Sonata 3

47217

Allegro

Double Bass

SCHIRMER'S LIBRARY
OF MUSICAL CLASSICS

Vol. 1898

BENEDETTO MARCELLO

Six Sonatas
For Cello or Double Bass and Piano

Double Bass part edited by
LUCAS DREW

ISBN 978-0-7935-5180-4

G. SCHIRMER, Inc.

DISTRIBUTED BY

HAL•LEONARD®
CORPORATION
7777 W. BLUEMOUND RD. P.O. BOX 13819 MILWAUKEE, WI 53213

NOTE

The following interpretive suggestions may be considered by the performer of the version for Double Bass:

1. The slow movements are similar to arias and are played with a smooth, sustained sound.

2. In general, sixteenth notes in the fast movements are played detachè (a smooth stroke with the bow pressed firmly into the string) while eighth notes are usually interpreted as martelè (a clean stop between each note, but not too short).

3. Dynamics often follow the contour of the melodic passages within the range of the printed, general dynamic level.

4. Embellishments have been included by the editor, but may be augmented or in a few places deleted.

It is hoped that this edition will be helpful in viewing the *Six Sonatas* as a unit.

LUCAS DREW

Bass

Solo Bass Part
edited by Lucas Drew

Six Sonatas
for Violoncello (or Bass) and Piano

Benedetto Marcello
(1686-1739)

Sonata 1

Largo

f (second time *p*)

f (second time *p*)

Allegro

f

p

f

*may be interpreted as

47217cx

Sonata 2

Allegro moderato

Sonata 3

Adagio

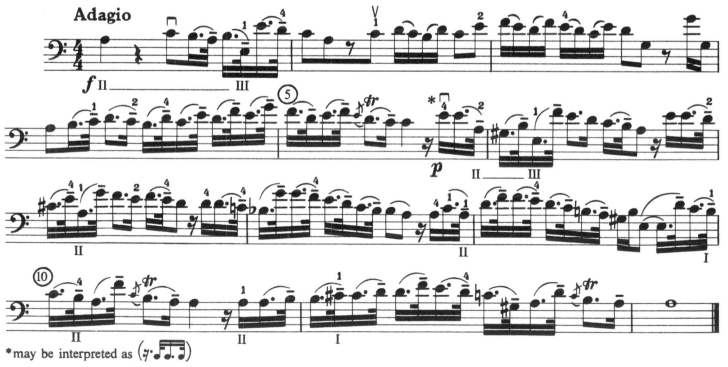

*may be interpreted as $\left(\gamma \cdot \, \boxed{} \right)$

Sonata 4

Bass

Sonata 5

Bass

Sonata 6

Bass

Cello

SCHIRMER'S LIBRARY
OF MUSICAL CLASSICS

Vol. 1898

BENEDETTO MARCELLO

Six Sonatas
For Cello or Double Bass and Piano

Keyboard Realization and
Cello part edited by
ANALEE BACON

ISBN 978-0-7935-5180-4

G. SCHIRMER, Inc.

DISTRIBUTED BY

HAL•LEONARD®
CORPORATION
7777 W. BLUEMOUND RD. P.O. BOX 13819 MILWAUKEE, WI 53213

Six Sonatas

for Violoncello (or Bass) and Piano

Violoncello

Solo Violoncello Part
edited by Analee Bacon

Benedetto Marcello
(1686~1739)

Sonata 1

47217 cx

Sonata 2

Sonata 3

Violoncello

Sonata 4

Violoncello

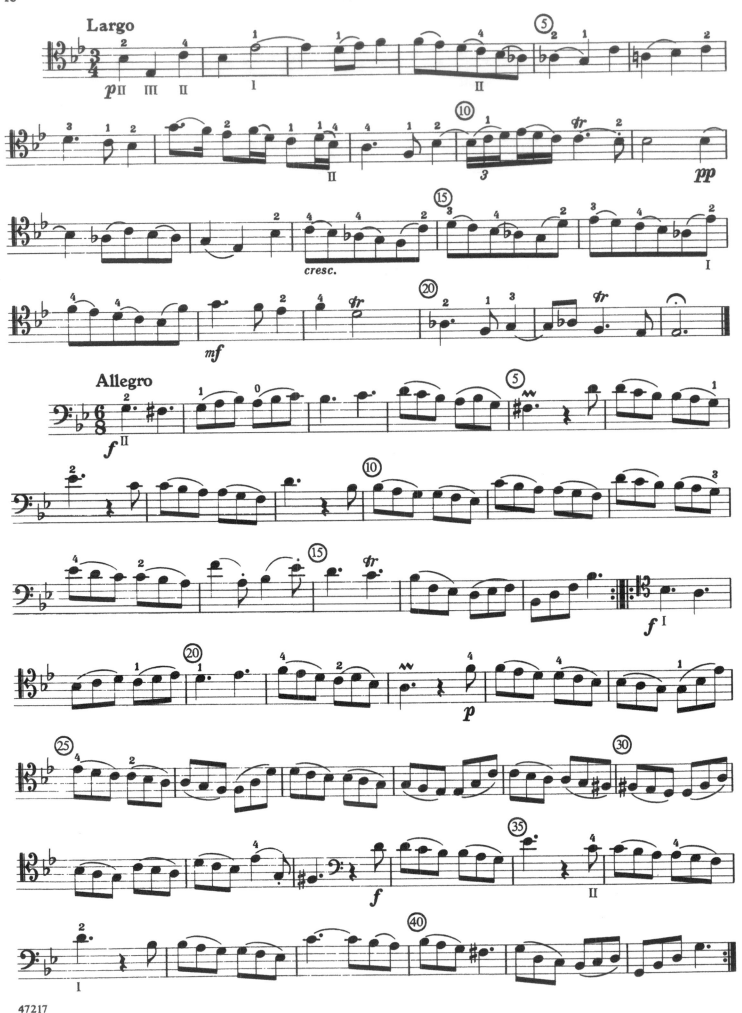

Sonata 5

Violoncello

Sonata 6

Violoncello

Sonata 4

Sonata 5

Adagio

Sonata 6

Adagio